Seasonal Table Settings

21 Designs Inspired by Nature

Catharina Lindeberg-Bernhardsson
Photos by Roland Persson

Schiffer Publishing Ltd

4880 Lower Valley Road   Atglen, Pennsylvania 19310

Other Schiffer Books on Related Subjects:
Table Decor, 0-7643-2472-1, $24.95

Library of Congress Control Number: 2011942938

Type set in ITC Avant Garde

ISBN: 978-0-7643-4018-5
Printed in China

Schiffer Books are available at special discounts for bulk purchases for sales promotions or premiums. Special editions, including personalized covers, corporate imprints, and excerpts can be created in large quantities for special needs. For more information contact the publisher:

Published by Schiffer Publishing Ltd.
4880 Lower Valley Road
Atglen, PA 19310
Phone: (610) 593-1777; Fax: (610) 593-2002
E-mail: Info@schifferbooks.com

For the largest selection of fine reference books on this and related subjects, please visit our website at:
www.schifferbooks.com
We are always looking for people to write books on new and related subjects. If you have an idea for a book, please contact us at
proposals@schifferbooks.com

This book may be purchased from the publisher.
Include $5.00 for shipping.
Please try your bookstore first.
You may write for a free catalog.

In Europe, Schiffer books are distributed by
Bushwood Books
6 Marksbury Ave.
Kew Gardens
Surrey TW9 4JF England
Phone: 44 (0) 20 8392 8585; Fax: 44 (0) 20 8392 9876
E-mail: info@bushwoodbooks.co.uk
Website: www.bushwoodbooks.co.uk

Contents

Decorate the table guided by the season and your taste. Be inspired!

There is almost nothing more welcoming than a beautifully set table and it is so easy to arrange. You will find twenty-one suggestions for settings in this book, all beginning with the bounty of each season: flowers, vegetables, and everything else in nature.

I would like my table settings to inspire you to decorate in your own style and with what you have on hand, so go out in the woods, to the beach, or see what the garden has to offer. Gather everything in a basket. Also take a look at the farmer's market or in fruit stands. Choose whatever will contribute to a pretty table decoration; though, whenever possible, select organic and environmentally-friendly products.

Once you have your items in hand, you can either set the table directly or begin by laying a tablecloth that you like. After that, all you have to do is arrange the items you've picked out. With this book as a guide, you'll see how easy it is to have a fantastic table setting.

Sometimes the unexpected can be exciting. What about a roll of grass sod filled with fine spring flowers or a runner of moss on the table? If you add bowls of mushroom soup covered with moss to the table, it will be a success.

In this book you'll even find a setting where seed potatoes in a box are the main attraction. All you need are tea lights to complete the very effective — and recyclable — setting. Just plant the potatoes in the ground after the party is over.

Think in color when you set the table. Let the food and decorations complement each other. An asparagus risotto is set off by a green arrangement of, for example, limes, broccoli, and green beans.

Edible decorations! A table full of spices not only gives taste to the food, but also provides a topic of conversation — an important consideration if the guests don't know each other very well.

Table settings for important holidays also offer some surprises.

My hope with this book is that the welcoming table settings will inspire your own creations. So, my advice isn't to follow this book exactly, but to decorate as you like. For example, instead of leaves, use chestnuts, or stones instead of moss, etc. The settings should reflect your own personality.

Good luck!

Catharina

About thirty years ago a new type of cookbook started to pop up, which slowly but surely changed our views about cooking. Earlier we consulted endless recipe collections that we were expected to follow exactly without always really understanding what was involved. Now we could suddenly leaf through colorful and inspiring books filled with appetizing pictures and easy-to-understand recipes that home cooks could follow successfully.

It was emancipating. I have said it before and I'll say it again: the new style of cookbooks contributed hugely to the rapid development of the art of cooking during the last quarter century. They awakened interest. They stimulated creativity. They opened a floodgate. After that, there was no stopping this development.

Now Catharina Lindeberg-Bernhardsson, this lovely, somewhat bohemian, and very artistic woman, intends to achieve something similar within her specialty, an almost totally neglected part of the meal that remains after the cook has done her work: the experience around the table.

Leaf through this book and enjoy the pictures. They make me so happy that my mouth starts to water. To be precise, they aren't just about how to set the table. I would say that Catharina creates tables. The most fun aspect is that she invites everyone to follow her example. You can manage this with a little guidance. Look at the photos, read the short texts, and you'll see what I mean. Isn't it liberating, exhilarating, sensual?

"Take in everything around you," says Catharina. "Enjoy the beauty of fruits, vegetables, and plants of all sorts. Let yourself be seduced. Make the table as irresistible and inviting as the food you are serving."

I would like to add to this thought: imagine the moment when your guests sit down around a table loaded with pumpkins, green tomatoes, red-yellow apples, romanesco and broccoli (Roman cauliflower), ivy, pea pods, rose hips, some green spruce leaves, a little mossy-colored moss and, at the center of everything, some delicious smelling grilled food or whatever the cook has found for the evening. Judging by the experience of Catharina's privileged guests — as I have often been — it will be a totally new type of meal that neither you nor the guests will forget quickly, I promise.

Guest Lars Arvid Boisen

SPRING

Valentine's Day

Valentine's Day, February 14, is a relatively new tradition in Sweden, where it is also known as All Hearts Day, and it calls for a romantic and intimate dinner in red and pink. Of course, this setting and decoration scheme would be suitable for any other occasion in which you want to show appreciation or celebrate your nearest and dearest, including Baptisms, birthdays, and weddings, to name but a few.

MATERIALS
~ 2 heart-shaped oasis dry foam blocks, a large solid one and a small heart with open center (available at hobby shops)
~ gold-colored lining material for the tablecloth
~ green rose leaves
~ thick floral wire
~ red roses, preferably two different shades
~ orange velvet ribbon
~ white roses
~ cherries
~ pink tulle ribbon
~ white linen napkins
~ grapes
~ oasis dry foam block and sphere
~ pink roses
~ dark cerise carnations

SETTING THE TABLE
~ Place the dry foam in water. Begin the table arrangement with a gold-colored cloth and then put out gold-edged china, silverware, champagne flutes, and water glasses.
~ Now let's decorate the foam oasis. Take the green rose leaves and lay them out so they overlap slightly. Bend a piece of floral wire and stick it in the sides of the oasis. Attach the groups of rose leaves to the floral wire all around so that they cover the edges.
~ Trim the stalks of the red roses so that they are about ¾" (or 2 cm.) long. Cover the heart with red roses. If you have chosen a couple of colors, mix them.
~ Finish by tying the orange ribbon around the floral wire. Secure the ribbon at the tip of the heart with a bit of the wire.
~ Stick the white roses into the smaller, open center oasis heart, spacing them evenly.
~ Now put in the cherries, which you have first skewered with a small piece of floral wire. Place the cherries in and around the heart.
~ Finish with a pink tulle ribbon — tie it into a rosette, leaving long tails. Bend a piece of wire through the knot and secure at the tip of the heart.
~ Fold the white linen napkins and place a rose and some grapes in each. Finish by strewing rose petals over the table for a lovely setting.

ROSES AND GRAPES IN COPPER
A copper dish is an excellent vessel for a romantic decoration with grapes and roses. Place a dampened oasis block in the dish. Cover with dark red grapes, trim the rose stems to about 3/4" (or 2 cm.), and place them evenly spaced out among the grapes.

LOVER'S BALL
Stick carnations and roses into the dampened dry foam sphere, covering the whole ball with flowers. This looks lovely on a table with a white tablecloth — and is even lovelier to give away!

Environmental Table Settings

When I was out walking in the fields and saw the farmers planting seed potatoes, I thought how unbelievably beautiful it was with all the potato boxes. I must set my table with that! Said and done. I talked to a farmer, who generously put a box of potatoes in my car. Of course, you must serve organic food to go with a table decorated by a box of potatoes. (See pages 22-23)

MATERIALS
~ natural fiber table cloth, dark green
~ china
~ organic seed potatoes in a box
~ tea lights
~ rhubarb leaves
~ natural fiber dish cloths, assorted colors

SETTING THE TABLE
~ Spread out the tablecloth.
~ Set the table with pretty white china.
~ Place the potato box at the center of the table or on one side. If you are having several guests, you can set out several potato boxes.
~ Put tea lights in among the potatoes! This simplicity enhances their beauty.
~ Lay a pretty rhubarb leaf on each plate.
~ Fold the dishcloths to use as napkins.

DECORATING TIP
Make a still life by mixing the seed potatoes with some tender rhubarb leaves in a bowl. See page 21.

"I planted the seed potatoes that were the decorations for my student exam party and am now waiting for my own potato harvest. That's what I call re-cycling."

Anything Is Possible!

Take the grass inside and lay it on the table! I have seldom experienced such an "aha-moment" as when I rolled a grass mat onto a newly ironed damask tablecloth.

The best food to go with this setting would be spring chicken and early vegetables, followed by a refreshing dessert with lime halves to squeeze over it.

MATERIALS
~ fine white tablecloth
~ aluminum foil
~ rubber gloves
~ 1 roll grass sod (2-1/5 yards x 15-3/4" (2 x .40 m) — the size of your table will determine the amount of sod you'll need. Several rolls can be laid out one after the other.
~ spring flowers (daisies and/or pansies)
~ limes (optional)
~ white china
~ white napkins
~ potted violets

SETTING THE TABLE
~ Lay out a freshly ironed pretty tablecloth
~ Arrange the foil like a runner down the whole table
~ Put on the rubber gloves
~ Bring the grass sod to the table and begin rolling it out where the foil starts.
~ Cut little crosses in the grass where you want to set the flowers.
~ Fold the grass up a bit and place the flowers into the crosscuts. Press down lightly. "Plant" the remaining flowers in the grass the same way, spreading them out over the mat.
~ It might be nice to have just one color of flower, for example, only white.
~ Halve the limes and place the halves at different places on the grass. (The limes aren't necessary, but they provide a lovely scent and accent color.)
~ Set the table with the white china
~ Fold the napkins like a candle holder and fold down the points of the fabric like flower petals, and then place a little pot into each napkin.
~ Put the glasses on the grass to lighten up the atmosphere and set the tone.

<small>OPPOSITE PAGE:</small> Violets in a napkin.

Easter Dinner

Here's how I set the table for Easter dinner at a friend's house using her grandmother's beautiful hand-painted china. The table was set with a real bird's nest that I found in the garden. I put some china eggs into the nest.

MATERIALS
~ burlap sacking (available from garden shops)
~ long sprays of weeping birch
~ floral wire
~ hay *(or sisal in case some of the guests are allergic to hay)
~ brown and white eggs, uncooked and boiled
~ small white feathers, preferably quail
~ little decorative chickens
~ daffodils
~ natural-colored linen napkins

SETTING THE TABLE
~ Spread out the tablecloth. If you want the cloth to reach the floor, you just have to lay out two lengths of burlap sacking next to each other and then cover the split with a third length. This is particularly nice if you are setting the table for a buffet.
~ Make the bird's nest. Begin by winding long sprays of weeping birch several times around to make the shape of a bird's nest. Finish by securing the branches with some floral wire.
~ Put a little hay in the center — this is where you will lay the eggs and egg shells.
~ Crack some of the raw eggs. Remove the contents and rinse the shells well. Place the shells randomly around the hay. Several shells grouped onto one branch makes a nice effect. Also spread out the feathers and little chickens in the nest and on the table.
~ Let the guests contribute to the decorations by painting the boiled eggs and placing the painted eggs on the table. Later each guest can choose an egg suiting their tastes and preferences.
~ Now bring out some serving dishes (i.e. coffee pots, creamers, and sugar bowls) and put daffodils in them.
~ Roll the napkins and shape them into nests. Place a boiled egg in each napkin nest and write the guest's name on the egg so that the seating arrangement is in order!

Herring, salmon, lamb, eggs, and an omelet are on the Easter menu, of course!

"I can leave the ironed tablecloths in the linen cupboard and buy some burlap sacking instead."

Little Easter

I call this setting "Little Easter" because it is so simple to do. Of course, it works equally well for the "big" Easter dinner, too. I used hand-painted cups for the coffee after dinner.

MATERIALS
~ burlap sacking
~ hay *(or sisal in case some of the guests are allergic to hay)
~ daffodils with bulbs, in plastic pots
~ clay pots
~ moss
~ uncooked eggs

SETTING THE TABLE
~ Spread the burlap over the table. Spread out the hay like a table runner.
~ Put the daffodils into the clay pots and cover with moss.
~ Line up the pots along the hay.
~ Crack some of the uncooked eggs and remove the contents.
~ Rinse the egg shells well and decorate the table with them.

COVERED POTS
~ Wrap brown wrapping paper around a clay pot (another type of pot will also work since the paper will hide the pot).
~ Put a little hay in the pot.
~ Press down an egg shell containing a daffodil and bulb, or stick a daffodil with a stalk down into a bit of oasis dry foam that you place in the pot.
~ Fill in with some bird seed.

MATERIALS
~ brown wrapping paper
~ clay pots
~ hay *(or sisal in case some of the guests are allergic to hay)
~ daffodils with bulbs or daffodils with stalks
~ egg shells
~ oasis dry foam
~ bird seed

A Colorful Easter

I've chosen a purple tablecloth for this setting because purple is one of my favorite colors. Feel free to choose the color scheme you prefer. When it comes to the feathers, you can select many different colors or just one, a choice that is often quite effective.

MATERIALS
~ brightly colored tablecloth
~ feathers in assorted colors
~ clay pots (other types of pots will work just as well)
~ whortleberries (or another type of twiggy berry plant)
~ cloth napkins (should be the same color as the tablecloth)

SETTING THE TABLE
~ Spread out the tablecloth. Fill the pots with feathers, with only one color of feather in each pot. If the feathers are placed in with the whortleberries, then use several different colors in the pot.

CARNATIONS IN A POT
Carnations in a pot would be an excellent addition to this table setting.

~ Place a dampened oasis block in a pot.
~ Trim the carnation stalks to about 2" or 5 cm.
~ Stick the carnations into the foam block.
~ Shape the carnations into a ball sticking out of the pot.
~ Use roses instead of carnations if you prefer.

MATERIALS
~ clay pots
~ oasis dry foam block
~ carnations

Pretty Table Decorations

A decorative wreath and a covered pot will look good on the table or place them to one side where they can be seen.

EASTER TABLE WREATH

MATERIALS
~ round oasis foam (available from floral supply or hobby shops)
~ green leaves, whatever kinds you like
~ roses
~ carnations
~ pussy willows
~ limes
~ bamboo skewers
~ uncooked eggs

WHAT TO DO
~ Put a round oasis foam block into some water.
~ Trim the leaf stems until there is about 1-1/2" (or 4 cm.) of stalk left. Stick the leaf stems into the foam block. The leaves should cover the block completely.
~ Trim the rose, carnation, and pussy willow stems to about 2" (5 cm.), and then stick the flower stems and stalks into the wreath.
~ Halve the limes and insert a skewer into each half. Stick the skewer down into the foam so that the cut edges of the limes are facing up.
~ Crack the eggs and reserve the contents. Rinse the shells. Place the egg shells around the edges of the wreath and the whole eggs at the center.

PANSIES IN A MOSS-COVERED POT

This looks absolutely beautiful on a dinner table covered with a purple cloth.

MATERIALS
~ floral wire
~ moss
~ potted pansies

WHAT TO DO
~ Cover some floral wire with moss. Make sure it stays secure.
~ Wind the moss around the pot with pansies.

Dinner in the Spirit of the Woods

The woods are our theme. We will go out and pick a bit of the woods to put on the table. We can inhale the woodsy smell when we drink a lovely mushroom soup through the moss!

MATERIALS
~ burlap sacking (available in packets at garden shops)
~ aluminum foil
~ green moss (pick some or buy)
~ flowering plants (assorted colors of pansies, crocuses, violas, and wood anemones)
• drinking straws
• white cloth napkins

SETTING THE TABLE
~ First cover the table with the burlap.
~ Next, use the foil to cover the areas on the table where you'll place the moss to protect the table and cloth.
~ Put the moss on top of and down the foil strips.
~ Now press some flowers down into the moss.
~ Set the table with white china as a contrast so all the flower colors will stand out.
~ Complete the effect of a natural dinner setting with white cloth napkins.

Invite your guests for some mushroom soup. You can serve the soup in an unusual way by covering each soup bowl with foil and then covering the foil with moss and inserting a straw through the moss/foil. This allows the guests to suck up the soup and the mushroom taste, as their olfactory senses get their share of the woods by smelling the moss.

"The table setting as inspiration for conversation is nothing new. In the past, people used 'figurines' for describing events to converse about. Now we can cover the table with moss, spices, vegetables, fruit, and anything else that gives a little taste of the season — and that also can lead to exciting conversations."

Woodland Buffet

A buffet is a great way to serve a meal!

A buffet makes an impression when there is a dramatic setting. When you invite some guests that don't know each other, a buffet is a great solution. The guests can talk with each other while they get their food and, if they have trouble finding topics of conversation, they can always talk about the exciting table setting.

For my buffet I've chosen an odd table made of driftwood and opted not to use a tablecloth. Of course, it will work just as well with a regular or glass table.

MATERIALS
~ newspaper
~ moss
~ potted herbs
~ strawberries
~ tomatoes on a stem
~ limes
~ flowers (i.e. pansies)
~ weeping birch sprays
~ floral wire
~ heavy cloth napkins

"Every time I take a walk I see all sorts of things I can set the table with."

SETTING THE TABLE
~ Begin by covering the table with newspaper or something else to protect the table top. Now lay out some moss.
~ Spread out the potted herbs.
~ Make little piles of strawberries, tomatoes, and limes.
~ Arrange the flowering plants among the vegetables.
~ Put all the food that will be served directly on the moss so it looks like a picnic on the grass. You can even let the guests pick and eat the decorative piles.
~ Put the bread in a basket that you've made of weeping birch branches. Here's how you make the basket: Shape a wreath from the branches and secure with a piece of floral wire. Put the wreath on the table and cover the hole with a cloth napkin. Put the bread into the napkin.

SUMMER

Wedding Dinner in the Country

Here's a table setting that is not only suitable for a wedding, but also any other special party, i.e. a fiftieth birthday or dinner with friends and relatives. The pictures show the table set with my great-grandmother's china and silverware. Though I didn't do it here, a fantastic alternative would be to use an assortment of flowers and colors for your table setting!

MATERIALS
~ white tablecloth
~ remay cloth (available at gardening centers)
~ oasis foam block
~ Savoy cabbage
~ bamboo skewers
~ white roses
~ limes
~ fennel
~ white place cards edged with gold

SETTING THE TABLE:
~ Spread out the white tablecloth and then lay the remay cloth over the white cloth. Voilà! Very effective!
~ Now put out the Savoy cabbages, some as is and some decorated (see below).

Now's the season for the first new potatoes, early spring vegetables, and prime veal… A menu idea perhaps?

DECORATED SAVOY CABBAGE
~ Put the foam block in water. Scoop out a round hole about 4" (10 cm.) in diameter and about 1-1/4" (3 cm.) deep in the center of the cabbage head.
~ Cut the foam block to fit the hole in the cabbage and place it in the hole.
~ Stick one or two skewers down in the center of the foam to secure it. Trim the skewers flush with the edge of the block.
~ Trim ten rose stems to about 1" (2.5 cm.) and stick them into the foam block, spacing them evenly around.
~ Halve the limes, stick a skewer through the peel of each half, trim the skewer to about 1-1/4" (3 cm.) and place the lime halves in with the roses.
~ Stand a fennel bulb with a place card on each of the heavy cloth napkins.

Remay cloth, normally used to cover and protect potato
plants in the spring, is used here for the table setting.

Early Summer Dinner

It is so wonderful when we can begin sitting outside late into the evenings. For this setting, I've covered the table with a sand-colored linen tablecloth. Of course, the setting will work equally well with a cloth in another pale color such as linden flower green or lavender.

MATERIALS
~ sand-colored tablecloth and cloth napkins
~ 2 oasis foam spheres (available in hobby or flower shops)
~ 2 pillar candles
~ white chrysanthemums
~ small bouquets of lily of the valley
~ twine

SETTING THE TABLE
~ Spread the cloth over the table.
~ Put the oasis foam in water. The spheres should be heavily saturated with water so they will be steady for holding candles. Take one of the pillar candles and press it slightly against the foam to mark the size of the candle. Use a knife to cut a hole the size of the marking. Put the candle into the hole. Prepare the other oasis sphere the same way.
~ Trim the chrysanthemum stems to about 1-1/4" to 1-1/2" (3-4 cm.) and stick the flowers into the spheres, spacing them very closely all over the ball. Put each ball into a discrete dish so that the water won't run out.
~ Wrap twine around each bouquet of lily of the valley. If you are setting the table for a dinner party, you can tie the place cards into one end of the twine.
~ Fold the napkins simply and place a bouquet on top of each napkin.

Chicken with fresh vegetables would be an excellent choice to go with this table setting.

Coffee & Tea on a Summer Afternoon

Cornflowers and oxeye daisies are about as summery as you can get. Whortleberries are sometimes the best to decorate with. The berry has a lovely light green color and covers extremely well.

MATERIALS
~ lace tablecloth or yardage
~ oasis foam wreath
~ whortleberries
~ cornflowers
~ oxeye daisies
~ cloth napkins
~ strawberries
~ bouquet of meadow flowers

SETTING THE TABLE
~ Spread the cloth over the table.
~ Dampen the oasis foam wreath.
~ Stick the whortleberries into the wreath to cover it. Trim the flower stems and stick them into the foam randomly.
~ Put a cloth napkin in the hole at center of wreath and pile the buns on top of the napkin.
~ Decorate the table by strewing strawberries and flower bouquets directly on the table.
~ Make a summery impression by using unmatched cups and saucers. This is also trendy in these days of recycling.
~ A footed serving dish would be quite pretty for holding the strawberries or a nice summer cake.

For a dinner with a similar table setting, you can put out small bouquets for each guest, perhaps with a place card inserted. You can pick the little bouquets of summer flowers yourself.

Dancing Sweet Peas

I love this table setting! Go out and pick bunches of whortleberries.

MATERIALS
• white table cloth and cloth napkins
• whortleberries
• water tubes (available in hobby and flower shops)
• floral wire
• sweet peas, assorted colors
• thin tulle ribbon

SETTING THE TABLE
• Spread the cloth over the table.
• Pick bunches of whortleberries and turn them upside down.
• Put a water tube into each bunch and wrap with floral wire.
• Fill the little tube with water and put in some sweet peas. Totally easy!
• Fold the white napkins and tie with some ribbon. Put a sweet pea under the ribbon.

I suggest nettle quiche served with cold smoked salmon to go with this setting.

FALL

Harvest Feast

No matter where you live, you'll be able to find all the ingredients for this table decoration. Whether it's at the farmer's market, in the garden, or in the woods, everything is ripe and ready to be harvested. So, set the table for the harvest feast!

MATERIALS

~ 6-1/2 yards (6 m) sacking (available in garden shops)
~ 5-1/4 yards (5 m) lime-colored velvet fabric (choose a quality to suit your taste and budget)
~ rose hips
~ some spruce branches (optional but recommended)
~ broccoflower
~ broccoli
~ pea pods
~ cauliflower – several colors
~ Brussels sprouts
~ tomatoes – yellow, red, and green
~ red cabbage
~ broccoli romanesco (Roman cauliflower)
~ green onions
~ apples
~ pears
~ kale
~ natural colored napkins
~ lion-yellow curtain tassels

SETTING THE TABLE

~ This table is set for four, but you can arrange the settings to fit in as many as ten guests. Begin by cutting the sacking and the fabric cloth down the center, to make three pieces each 2-3/4 yards (2.5 m) long.
~ Spread the sack cloth over the table. The sacking gives a feeling of the harvest. Next, spread out the two lengths of velvet.
~ Now you have a pretty base for decorating. Place the vegetables and fruits out like a runner. Begin with the rose hips and leaves scattered here and there. Use the kale to finish the "runner" at both ends.
~ Arrange small piles of vegetables, some of each one in every pile. Put the biggest piles at the center of the runner.
~ Set out the soup bowls.
~ Twist the napkins around the bowls and secure them with the curtain tassels.

"Setting an inspiring table feels like the absolutely most important item in every party arrangement."

Use peapods as place cards and write the
names using black ink.

Here's a suggestion for using a seedling
pot for the place cards!

NAPKIN CANDLE WITH APPLE
Fold the napkin like a candle; turn down one edge and place an apple on top.
Write the names on small tags, thread on a cord, and securely tie the tags to the
apple stem.

Autumn Buffet

It's not just vegetables and fruits that light up the table here, but also the food that will be served. The food provides color sparks all over the "rough" setting.

MATERIALS
~ sacking (available in gardening shops) – enough to cover the table and reach the floor
~ hay *(or sisal in case some of the guests are allergic to hay)
~ apples
~ tomatoes, preferably in several colors
~ Brussels sprouts
~ Swedish turnips
~ red cabbage
~ cauliflower, preferably in several colors
~ onions, both purple and green
~ frisee (curly-edged) lettuce
~ brown eggs, organic recommended
~ kale
~ black radishes
~ broccoli romanesco (Roman cauliflower)
~ French beans
~ sunflowers

SETTING THE TABLE
~ Spread out the sacking so that it covers the table and reaches down to the floor. Lay hay or some lovely fall leaves all over. Alternately, you can leave the sacking "as is."
~ Decorate with the piles of fruits and vegetables you've selected. Arrange the piles so that the guests can take what they like from the décor.
~ Put out the buffet food between the piles of fruit and vegetables. If there is room, you can also set out the plates and silverware on the table.
~ If you have time, the desire, and the space, you can make a still life of vegetables at the center of the table. Think about creating a pretty color mix.
~ Finish by laying the sunflowers on the buffet table as points of light.

"Catharina relieved me of the notion that you have to decorate sparingly. Just the opposite, you can think big and experiment with grass, leaves, vegetables, flowers, and hay (or sisal if some of the guests are allergic to hay)."

Eat the Table Setting!

Use the food for the table decoration. It adds some extra spice to set the conversation going when everyone picks out something to eat from the setting – would you please pass me a little basil? Of course you'll serve organic food with this setting.

MATERIALS
~ second-hand tablecloth (the photo shows an old curtain)
~ hay *(or sisal in case some of the guests are allergic to hay)
~ potted herbs
~ glasses, assorted colors
~ cardstock
~ clothes pins
~ plates, preferably with different patterns

SETTING THE TABLE
~ Lay a cloth over the table if you want to use one.
~ Spread out the hay like a table runner at the center of the table.
~ Place the potted herbs in a row, setting the pots into the hay.
~ Set the table with various colors of glasses that match the other colors on the table.
~ Write the guests' names on pieces of cardstock and attach them to the plates with the clothes pins.

"With the potted herbs on the table, there was a mad rush as all the guests tried to pick out their favorites."

CABBAGE POT.
Trim a red cabbage. Carve a hole in the top and put a plant into the hole.

Colorful Cauliflowers in a Row

This setting is quite minimal, but so very pretty with all the colorful cabbages! A nice broccoli soup will go well with this table setting.

MATERIALS
~ cauliflowers, purple, orange, and white
~ broccoli stalks
~ clay pots
~ hay *(or sisal in case some of the guests are allergic to hay)
~ white ink pen
~ black cardstock
~ thin cord

SETTING THE TABLE
~ Put the colored cauliflowers and broccoli stalks into clay pots.
~ Line up the pots down the center of the table for a nice effect.
~ If you want, you can begin by filling the pots with hay and then put in the broccoli stalks and cauliflowers.
~ Make the place cards. Write the guests' names with white ink on black pieces of cardstock and attach the cardstock to the silverware with a fine cord.

"I always think in color when I set the table these days. I can choose to set with whatever is on hand as long as the colors harmonize."

Simple Fall Setting

Fall is a fantastically inspiring season for table settings. There are leaves in every color imaginable (red, yellow and green) and ripe fruits, berries, and vegetables ready to be harvested. You just have to go get them!

This simple fall table setting makes a pretty buffet table. All the food to be served can be set out on the "leaf cloth."

MATERIALS
~ basket full of leaves in every color and shape imaginable
~ medium-size apples (organic recommended)
~ pears (organic recommended)
~ walnuts (organic recommended)
~ rose hips
~ napkins

SETTING THE TABLE
~ Cover the table with leaves.
~ Spread out the fruits and nuts over the table.
~ Finish by setting the plates on the "leaf cloth."
~ Fold the napkins into triangles, roll them a few turns and then fold at the center.
~ Place a leaf and a fork and knife in each napkin.

APPLES IN A POT
~ Dampen an oasis foam block and place it in a pot so that it comes up to the edge.
~ Stick a skewer into one end of an apple and then stick the skewer down into the foam block.
~ Do the same with the remaining apples until you've filled the pot.
~ Finish by topping with a bit of hay if you like.

MATERIALS
~ oasis dry foam block
~ clay pot
~ apples
~ 2" (5 cm.) long bamboo skewers
~ a little hay or sisal

Halloween Party

A little spooky party always helps to light up the fall gloom. This frightening table setting is just what we want!

MATERIALS
~ black tarp
~ orange fabric
~ black napkins (buy some yardage of black fabric and cut out the required number of napkins, they don't have to be hemmed, just washed!)
~ skeleton hands
~ garlic heads
~ plastic candleholders
~ black candles
~ spider webbing (available in hobby shops)
~ plastic spiders
~ black cardstock
~ white ink pen
~ 4 small pumpkins
~ 1 large pumpkin
~ plastic teeth
~ "bleeding" candles (optional, available in hobby shops)

SETTING THE TABLE
~ Spread the black tarp over the table and then lay the orange fabric over it.
~ Set out the plates, glasses, and silverware.
~ Roll the napkins. Put a little piece of orange fabric in some of the napkins and a skeleton hand in the others.
~ Arrange several garlic heads at the center of the table and spread out the rest.
~ Press a candleholder into the center of each garlic head and then put in the black candles.
~ Carefully cover the whole table with the spider webbing.
~ Attach the "spiders" to the webbing!
~ Cut wings out of the black cardstock. Write the guests' names on the wings. Carve a slit into each side of the small pumpkins and put a wing at the sides of each pumpkin. Now the place cards are ready.
~ Carve out a face on the large pumpkin. It doesn't have to be pretty as everyone knows! Embellish the pumpkin with a plastic spider. The plastic teeth and bleeding candles add to the spookiness.

A winged pumpkin becomes a place card.

Frightening table decorations.

Decorated Pumpkin

MATERIALS

~ one large pumpkin
~ oasis dry foam block
~ bamboo skewers
~ an assortment of flowers
~ ivy
~ apples
~ green tomatoes

WHAT TO DO

~ Cut the top off of the pumpkin and remove the seeds.
~ Place a piece of the oasis foam down in the hole and stick a skewer through it so that it stays steady. Trim the skewer flush with the oasis.
~ Arrange the flowers and ivy in the foam.
~ Skewer the apples and tomatoes. Stick the in skewers around the edges and above the foam. Finish by attaching the pumpkin top: stick two shortened skewers into the edge of the pumpkin and then press the lid onto the skewers (make sure that the piece remains steady).
~ Place the decorated pumpkin on the table or take it along as a gift that will be appreciated!

WINTER

White Mulled Wine Party

Here's a festive setting all in white and green for a glögg (mulled wine) party. Happy advent!

MATERIALS

~ insect netting (available in gardening shops)
~ aluminum foil
~ white moss
~ oasis dry foam block
~ white amaryllis (cut flowers)
~ flower stakes for amaryllis
~ white hyacinths with bulb
~ white poinsettias
~ white snowball candles
~ string of clear Christmas lights (battery-driven)
~ cinnamon sticks
~ hazelnuts
~ dried lime and orange slices
~ twigs (larch recommended)
~ glasses
~ mulled wine mugs

SETTING THE TABLE

~ Spread the netting over the table. Cover the center of the netting with foil and lay the white moss on top.
~ Make a still life in one corner of the table.
~ Arrange the flowers following the photos and text below.
~ Press the hyacinth bulbs and poinsettias down into the moss and then arrange the snowball candles the same way.
~ String the clear, battery-driven Christmas lights over the table. The table will be finely set with lights.
~ Spread out the cinnamon sticks, hazelnuts, and dried lime and orange slices over the table.
~ Make a little frame with the twigs.
~ Place the glasses and mugs in the moss!

Place the dampened oasis blocks on the foil. Take an amaryllis. Stick a flower stake through the hollow stalk and press the stake down into the foam. Cover with moss. Do the same with the remaining amaryllises. It will be especially pretty if you trim the amaryllises to different lengths.

"When I turn on the string of lights threaded through the moss on the Christmas table, I think of Catharina."

Hyacinth Wreath!

MATERIALS
~ hyacinths
~ hay wreath (frame for building up the wreath)
~ bamboo skewers
~ 1 white pillar candle
~ pine cones
~ cinnamon sticks
~ dried orange slices
~ hazelnuts

WHAT TO DO
~ Rinse the dirt off the hyacinth bulbs.
~ Stick the point of a bamboo skewer into a hyacinth bulb. Trim the skewer to desired length, about 1-1/2" (4 cm.), and push skewer into the wreath. Repeat with remaining hyacinths. They don't have to be spaced perfectly evenly; a little irregularity is rather nice.
~ Put a candle in the center of the wreath and then lay on some pinecones, cinnamon sticks, orange slices, hazelnuts, or whatever you like and have on hand.

A Christmassy Christmas Table

Nuts, fruits, pinecones, flowers, moss, and candles – yes, everything that belongs at Christmastime is here to decorate the table. All we have to do now is wish everyone a Very Merry Christmas! (See pages 120-121.)

MATERIALS
~ red velvet fabric (should be long enough to reach the floor on the short ends of the table)
~ plastic wrap
~ oasis dry foam blocks
~ flower stakes
~ red amaryllis
~ green moss
~ red apples
~ cinnamon sticks
~ pine cones
~ hazelnuts
~ dried lime and orange slices
~ gold paper
~ gold ribbon or cord
~ red cardstock
~ gold candles
~ red cloth napkins

SETTING THE TABLE
~ Cover the table with the red velvet fabric. The ends should reach the floor at least on the short sides of the table.
~ Lay a length of plastic wrap down the center of the table like a runner.
~ Place the dampened foam blocks evenly spaced down the plastic wrap.
~ Stick a flower stake into each amaryllis stalk (see page 111) and press them down evenly spaced into the foam blocks.
~ Cover with green moss.
~ Spread out the apples, cinnamon sticks, pinecones, hazelnuts, and lime and orange slices over the table.
~ Make a little packet with gold paper for each guest. Put an exciting little something into each packet or make just "pretend" packets. Tie with gold ribbon. Write the guest names on red cardstock and attach a name card to the ribbon on each package. Now the place cards are ready!
~ Put the gold candles in the candleholders.
~ Lay a folded napkin on each plate.

Table Wreath for Christmas

A large, generously decorated wreath with living light creates the Christmas spirit for this table. Red linen tablecloth, white china, and holly in clay pots complete the scene.

MATERIALS
~ round oasis dry foam wreath
~ branches of various conifer plants
~ assortment of wintergreen leaves
~ bamboo skewers
~ apples
~ red roses
~ floral wire
~ dried orange slices
~ pinecones
~ plastic candleholders
~ gold candles
~ red cloth napkins
~ potted holly plants
~ wood plant labels (used to label seedlings or plants)

SETTING THE TABLE
~ Cover the dampened foam block with conifer branches and wintergreen leaves.
~ Stick a skewer into an apple; trim the skewer to about 1-1/2" (4 cm.) and set the apple into the wreath. Repeat with remaining apples.
~ Trim the rose stems and stick down into the foam wreath.
~ Thread a short length of floral wire through two dried orange slices, twist the ends of the wire together, and press down into the foam. Do the same with the remaining orange slices.
~ Twist some floral wire around the pinecones and stick them into the wreath.
~ Finish by pushing the candleholders into the wreath, evenly spaced around. Put the gold candles into the holders.
~ Fold the red napkins lengthwise a couple of times and wrap each napkin around a little plastic pot with a holly plant. Write the guests' names on the wood plant labels and then put a pot onto each guests' plate.

Kale Decorations!

Thick green kale and young tulips... Fabulous!

MATERIALS
~ bunches of green kale
~ tulips with bulbs

SETTING THE TABLE:
~ Buy some bunches of kale and join them. Shape them by laying them on each other.
~ Stick the tulips with their bulbs in among the kale leaves. This will work with other flowers, but they must be bulb flowers or they will wilt quickly.

THANKS TO:

Lars Arvid Boisen

Py Wernstedt

Lena Forsman

Hedvig Stabell

Villeroy & Boch